BODY BITS

DEAD-AWESOME DINOSAUR BODY FACTS

by Paul Mason and Dave Smith

WAYLAND
www.waylandbooks.co.uk

First published in Great Britain in 2021 by Wayland

Text and illustrations copyright © Hodder & Stoughton, 2021

Editors: Grace Glendinning and Melanie Palmer
Designer: Peter Scoulding
Illustrations: Dave Smith

ISBN: 978 1 5263 1516 8 HBK

ISBN: 978 1 5263 1517 5 PBK

An imprint of
Hachette Children's Group
Part of Hodder & Stoughton

Carmelite House
50 Victoria Embankment
London EC4Y 0DZ

An Hachette UK Company
www.hachette.co.uk
www.hachettechildrens.co.uk

Printed in China

MIX
Paper from
responsible sources
FSC® C104740
FSC
www.fsc.org

Picture credits:
Alamy: Axis Images 7 cl; Stocktrek Images Inc 13bl, 13cr,
20, 23; World History Archive 6b. Shutterstock: Marcelo Alex 5br; Martina Badini
26; Ryan M Bolton 7 cr; Mark Bridger 17 cl; Dangdumrong 12; Digital Genetics 6t;
DM7 11bc, 17 b; Dotted Yeti 14r; Everett Collection 8b; Herschell Hoffmeyer 29;
Eric Isselee 8cr; A Ricardo 11br; Michael Rosskothen 13br, 27; stockphotomania
14l; Warpaint 28; Wildlife World 17 t. Wikimedia Commmons/CCA 3: H Raab 18.

Every attempt has been made to clear copyright. Should there be any
inadvertent omission please apply to the publisher for rectification.

The website addresses (URLs) included in this book were valid at the time of
going to press. However, it is possible that contents or addresses may have
changed since the publication of this book. No responsibility for any such
changes can be accepted by either the author or the Publisher.

INTELLIGENCE TEST
CLICK HERE TO START

Contents

Dinosaur domination 4

Teeth of terror 6

Clubs and horns 8

Hips and legs 10

Armour plates 12

Pea brains 14

Dino-vision eyes 16

Wings and similar things 18

Skin and feathers 20

Sails and spines 22

Dinosaur guts 24

Hooting and honking 26

The four freakiest dinosaurs? 28

Glossary 30

Finding out more 31

Index 32

Dinosaur domination

Dinosaurs lived on Planet Earth for more than 180 million years. For the last 79 million years of this, they ruled the planet.

Dinosaurs everywhere

Wherever you looked, there were dinosaurs. There were enormous ones that weighed as much as eight elephants, and tiny ones that weren't even as heavy as a hamster. Each dinosaur was adapted to the place it lived, what it ate and the predators it faced.

Pangaea breaks up

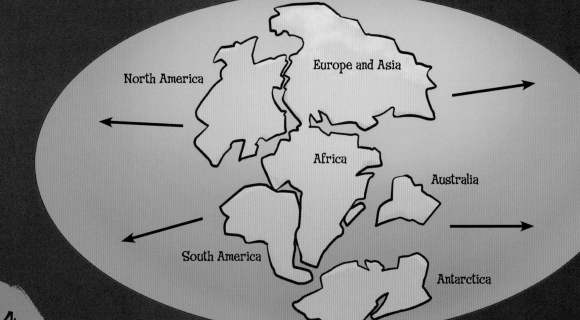

North America

Europe and Asia

Africa

Australia

South America

Antarctica

During the Jurassic Period, the huge area of land called Pangaea began to break up. Over millions of years, the pieces spread around the world. New habitats appeared, and dinosaur populations spread into each area.

Although the pieces of Pangaea eventually formed the continents we know today, back then the climate was MUCH warmer everywhere.

Dinosaur variety

The dinosaurs were very different from each other. Huge, long-necked sauropods wandered through the forests, stretching up for food. On the open plains, 'pursuit predators' like Afrovenator chased smaller dinosaurs, such as Spinostropheus. On the shores, crocodile-jawed Baryonyx and Spinosaurus hunted fish.

CHEW ... CHEW ... CHEW ...

Brachiosaurus had to eat about 300 kg of plants a day. No wonder its teeth were always wearing out.

The fastest dinosaurs were turkey-sized, and must have been very hard to catch.

AHHH!

Faster, Dorothy, faster!

Mystery body bits

The 500–600 species of dinosaur we know about today* had a wide variety of body bits – including many that we still don't fully understand. No one is sure why Spinosaurus had a sail on its back (though you can find out the most likely explanations in this book) or why Kosmoceratops had such fancy horns. For defence? Or to show off, a bit like a peacock?

SCIENCE FLASH

Experts usually work out what dinosaur body bits were for by comparing them to modern animals. For example, fast animals, such as cheetahs and ostriches, have longer legs, with a long lower part.

Ornithomimus had legs that fit these rules, and experts think it may have been able to run at over 50 kph.

Maybe a sunshade for the kids?

Or for hanging out the washing?

*New dinosaurs are being discovered every year, so this number changes all the time.

Teeth of terror

Dinosaurs had teeth that were adapted to all kinds of jobs, from grabbing fish to grinding plants. Some even had dagger-like teeth that really were DEAD awesome ...

No, I'm not a fussy eater.

As long as it's meat.

Meat-eater teeth

Dinosaurs from the Theropod family – most famous member: Tyrannosaurus rex (T. rex) – were predatory and often had long teeth with serrated edges (like a bread knife). They were good for biting and slicing.

Specialist teeth

Some predators had specialised teeth. Spinosaurus, for example, ate a LOT of fish. Its teeth were long and pointy, and fitted together. When Spinosaurus grabbed a big fish, it could not wriggle free.

Masiakasaurus hunted small, fast animals on land. It had lower teeth that stuck out forwards, which may not have looked very cute, but were ideal for grabbing its prey.

Interlocking teeth

Pressure sensor

Fishy movements spread out in waves in the water, and pressure sensors told Spinosaurus when there was prey nearby.

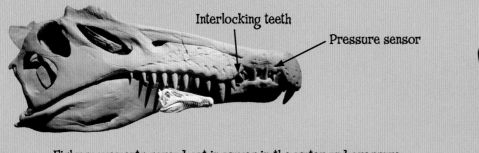

Those are SOME teeth!

Like I haven't heard THAT before!

Herbivore teeth

Dinosaurs that ate only plants are called herbivores. Their teeth were often wide and flat, like a Triceratops', for grinding tough stalks or woody stems. Other herbivorous dinosaurs had more-specialist teeth. Ankylosaurus, for example, had teeth designed for snipping plants.

We ate a plant-based diet before it was cool.

ANKYLOSAURUS TOOTH

TRICERATOPS TOOTH

Spoon-shaped with wide, sharp edges

Good for snipping off leaves

Thick and strong

Good for grinding down tough plants

Nigersaurus was like a dinosaur lawnmower. It had between 500 and 1,000 teeth, which it used for mowing up low-lying vegetation. Its teeth were constantly being worn out and lost.

Got any grass that needs cutting?

YEUW!

Nigersaurus is thought to have lost about 57 teeth per day ... which is 399 per week ... which is more than 1,700 teeth lost per MONTH!

Clubs and horns

In a world full of tyrannosaurs and other huge hunters, even a peace-loving plant-eater needed a little bit of flair and protection ...

Extreme horns and frills

Prize for 'fanciest horn' goes to Kosmoceratops. Its frill folded over and was edged with spikes. Kosmoceratops also had horns on its forehead, nose and cheeks.

Pentaceratops gets the prize for 'biggest horned skull': 3 m from tip to top (or about two Napoleons tall, if he stood on his own shoulders). Pentaceratops actually means 'five-horned face', though it didn't have five horns on its big skull*.

You call THAT a display?

Experts think the complex design to Kosmoceratops' frill might have been used to attract a mate, similar to a peacock's feathers.

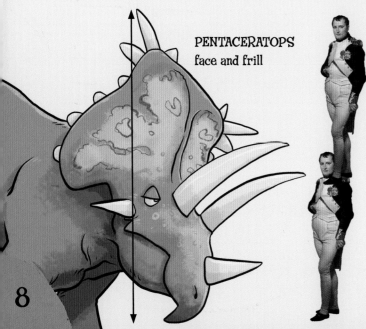

PENTACERATOPS
face and frill

NAPOLEON BONAPARTE:
emperor, commander ... but only about 1.7 m tall

The competition for 'longest horn' is a three-way split: Triceratops, Torosaurus and Coahuilaceratops all had horns up to about 1.2 m long. They could have made a nasty hole in the side of an attacking tyrannosaur.

*It had three horns, plus a bony spike under each eye.

8

GET LOST.

SWISH!

SWISH!

Tail clubs

Many dinosaurs had clubbed tails. They may have swished these from side to side as a way of keeping away attackers. The biggest, most famous of these dinosaurs is Ankylosaurus, which was so dangerous that experts think it could even have fought off a T. rex.

SCIENCE FLASH

Holding up a heavy club at the end of a bendy tail is tricky. The tail bones of club-tailed dinosaurs were stronger and stiffer than other dinos' tails. These tail bones are called the 'handle'. Strong muscles at the end of the handle allowed the dinosaur to whack attackers with bone-breaking force.

Ankylosaurus's tail club weighed about 50 kg – roughly seven bowling balls. It hardly moved up and down at all, but from side-to-side it could move about 50 degrees each way. It was like a built-in wrecking ball!

Hips and legs

Dinosaurs are descended from another kind of reptile, called an archosaur. The difference between the two was how their hips worked, which affected how they walked and ran.

Archosaur legs pointed outwards.

Running made it harder for archosaurs to breathe, as it squished their lungs.

They walked with a wide stance, like a crocodile's.

Dinosaur legs pointed downwards.

When dinosaurs ran, their lungs were not squished.

They walked with a narrower stance, similar to an ostrich's.

SCIENCE FLASH

Dinosaur hips are not only different to the archosaurs'. They can also be split into two main types:

- Lizard-hipped dinosaurs are called saurischians. The saurischians included predatory dinosaurs, such as Allosaurus, and large, long-necked ones, such as Apatosaurus.

- Bird-hipped dinosaurs are known as ornithischians. These dinosaurs included armoured and horny-headed dinosaurs, such as Tarchia and Stegosaurus.

Saurischian.

You take that back!

Dinosaur legs

Dinosaur legs worked in various ways. Giant titanosaurs (the biggest-ever dinosaurs, such as Argentinosaurus) needed huge, thick, strong legs to support their enormous bodies.

The small carnivore Deinonychus was much lighter and had longer, faster-moving (but still very strong) legs.

1 x Argentinosaurus

8 x African elephants

Grown man does not reach knees

50+ tonnes

As far as we know, Argentinosaurus was the heaviest dinosaur.

Argentinosaurus's great size meant that its legs could not move it forward very quickly. Its top speed was only about 10 kph – a lot slower than the fastest dinosaur, Compsognathus.

Compsognathus was about as big as a turkey and weighed only 2.5 kg.

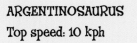

COMPSOGNATHUS
Top speed: 64 kph

ARGENTINOSAURUS
Top speed: 10 kph

ALLOSAURUS:
about 34 kph

Even big, predatory dinosaurs could run quite fast in short bursts. World-renowned sprinter Usain Bolt could have outrun Allosaurus, but an average 12-year-old could not.

BOLT:
nearly 45 kph

11

Armour plates

If your local predators are armed with teeth that look a bit like daggers, one way to protect yourself from their bite is to wear armour.

Quite a few plant-eating dinosaurs walked around in a permanent suit of armour. This armour wasn't metal, like a knight's – it was made of hard, bony scales or plates on their skin, which was difficult for predators to bite through.

Armoured dinosaurs had some of the most imaginative names of all the dinos*, such as Animantarx (Greek for 'living fortress') and Aletopelta ('wandering shield').

These armoured beasts were divided between ones with tail clubs and ones without.

SCIENCE FLASH

Dinosaur armour plating was made of osteoderms. These are bony deposits in an animal's skin, which many reptiles have today. Snakes, crocodiles, alligators, frogs and lizards all develop osteoderms. They provide protection and help keep the animal warm or cool.

Hoplitosaurus: no tail club
= a nodosaur

Euoplocephalus: tail club
= an ankylosaur

*Dinosaurs are named by either the person who discovers them or the palaeontologist who works out that they are a new, unknown species.

Eyelid armour

A tyrannosaur would have had to be feeling VERY hungry (or very hopeful) to attack Ankylosaurus: even Ankylosaurus *eyelids* had armour plating. It also had bony plates on its tail, back and shoulders.

Experts think Ankylosaurus also had a very good sense of smell, which would have helped it detect nearby predators.

Yes?

No, nothing, sorry.

Spiky welcome

Many armoured dinosaurs were protected not only by bony plates, but also by long spikes growing out of their skin.

Saichania had rows of large spikes just about everywhere except on its belly.

And Sauropelta had such a long spike on each shoulder that predators could not safely bite its neck without getting poked in the mouth.

Gastonia had spikes sticking out of its back, sides and tail.

Pea brains

Wait, what?

Dinosaur intelligence is tricky to estimate. We can compare Stegosaurus's brain to the size of a walnut, but just how well did that walnut work?

Small brains in big bodies

Most people know that dinosaurs had small brains compared to the size of their bodies. Scientists use brain size v. body size to work out roughly how intelligent an animal might be. Most experts think that even smart dinosaurs, such as Troodon, were probably only about as clever as a chicken.

SCIENCE FLASH

Dinosaurs evolved all kinds of new features to fit their surroundings. Some got bigger, others got faster or more dangerous, or better at catching particular prey. They may have evolved greater intelligence, but this did not happen quickly. This is because in a world of Mr Dafts, you only have to be Mr Not-Quite-So-Daft to be the cleverest dinosaur around.

Giant titanosaurs, with their huge bodies and tiny brains, were probably among the least-intelligent dinosaurs.

Were dinosaurs really daft?

The dinosaurs died out millions of years ago, long before humans appeared, so we cannot give them an intelligence test.

But we do share the planet with animals that are descended from dinosaurs: birds. Birds have miniature brains that are more powerful than their size suggests ... so maybe the pea-brained dinosaurs were sharper than people think ...

SCIENCE FLASH

Dinosaurs almost certainly gave their brains a rest by sleeping.* We don't know for sure how they slept, though. Were they lying down? Leaning against a tree? Cuddling a friend?

Mei long, a dinosaur discovered in China in 2004, appeared to be sleeping in a lying-down position. Other dinosaurs probably slept in different positions, depending on their body shapes and sizes.

*Modern-day reptiles don't sleep in exactly the same way as we do, but they do close their eyes and use their brains less.

SNORE!
SNORE!

Dinosaurs that might have slept standing up: stegosaurs, brachiosaurs.

Maybe slept in a sitting position: tyrannosaurs.

Arms too weak to push it upright if it laid down.

You probably wouldn't tell a tyrannosaur to stop snoring.

Maybe lying down: Triceratops, Procompsognathus, Velociraptor.

ZZzzzzz

15

Dino-vision eyes

One way to survive in the dino world was to see better than whatever was hunting you ... or whatever you were hunting.

Night-time hunters

Good dino-vision was especially important if, like some dinosaurs, you mostly hunted in the dark. Velociraptor and Deinonychus, for example, were probably night-time predators. We know this mainly because of two body bits: something called the scleral ring and the size of their eye sockets.

They can't see me ...

CREEP ...
CREEP...

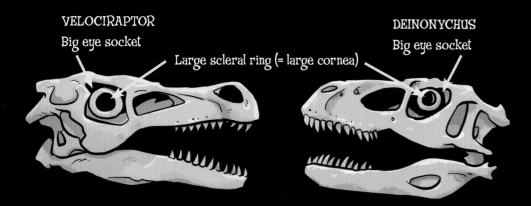

VELOCIRAPTOR
Big eye socket
Large scleral ring (= large cornea)

DEINONYCHUS
Big eye socket

Bigger eyes have larger corneas, the part of the eye that lets in light. This is very useful if you hunt by moonlight.

What's worse than meeting a Velociraptor? Meeting a Velociraptor in the dark! Although, Velociraptors weren't like the ones you've seen in films. In real life they were only the height of a turkey. If you met one in the dark, it would probably run away to avoid the giant human.

Dinosaurs were reptiles. Many of today's reptiles have eyes with slit pupils, so dinosaurs were historically drawn like this, too. Slit pupils can expand more than round ones to let in more light, so nocturnal dinosaurs might have had them.

Today we know that birds are descended from a group of dinosaurs called theropods – and birds have round pupils. So maybe some dinosaurs did, too?

Dinosaur pupils: circles or slits?

forward-facing eyes

The most famous predators in the dinosaur world were tyrannosaurs such as Albertosaurus, Gorgosaurus and T. rex. Many tyrannosaurs had forward-facing eyes, which gave them binocular vision. Experts think that a T. rex could probably see its prey even better than today's hawks and eagles.

On a clear day, T. rex could have seen objects clearly from almost 6.5 km away. And (despite what you may have seen in films), this definitely involved seeing things that weren't moving, too.

Wings and similar things

We know that some dinosaurs had wings (and feathers), but experts don't completely agree on whether or not they could actually fly.

Did this fossilised feather come from a bird or a dinosaur?

You're a dinosaur.

Um ... OK.

Seems a bit rude.

Archaeopteryx: the dino-bird

In 1861, a feather fossil was discovered in rock that formed over 145 million years ago. Experts named the animal the feather came from 'Archaeopteryx'. Everyone agreed at the time that Archaeopteryx must be a dinosaur. After all, birds (they thought) had not appeared on Earth until after the dinosaurs had died out.

Later, most* experts decided that Archaeopteryx was actually an early bird, not a dinosaur. Recently, scientists have studied Archaeopteryx's wing bones and discovered that the dino-bird could probably fly in short bursts, a bit like a pheasant.

But the discussion continues. Recently, a few experts have suggested that, although Archaeopteryx did have feathers, the feather that started it all actually came from a different dinosaur altogether.

*Not all experts agree ... Palaeontologists do love an argument.

Winged dinosaurs

Since Archaeopteryx, palaeontologists have discovered several dinosaur species with wings. They are not sure whether these dinosaurs could fly. Instead, they may have crawled up trees and waited for prey, before gliding down to attack.

YI QI

Recently, more winged dinosaurs have been found. In China, for example, Yi qi (whose name means 'strange wing' in Chinese) was discovered in 2015. It was mostly covered in feathers, but had bat-like wings, with thin skin stretched between long bones. It lived in woodland, possibly up in the trees.

Freaky four-wings

For some dinosaurs, two wings just weren't enough – they had four. Microraptor, for example, had wing-like feathery arms AND legs. With all those wings, some experts think Microraptor was able to fly. Microraptor hunted birds, and one fossil has been found with fish in its stomach.

Experts now think many dino feathers were a shiny black colour, including Microraptor's. So, sadly, our four-winged friend almost certainly wasn't orange.

skin and feathers

When dinosaurs were first discovered, people assumed that they looked like most modern reptiles. They drew dinosaurs with scaly green or brown skin like a crocodile's, but this may not be correct.

Not my style.

Too jazzy?

SCIENCE FLASH

Is there any evidence that dinosaurs had colourful skin? Yes, but only a tiny amount. Colour sacs in fossilised Sinosauropteryx feathers show that it was probably orange, with a stripy tail. And some sea reptiles that lived at the time of the dinosaurs also had colourful skin.

skin colour

Some modern reptiles have skin that is very brightly coloured. Coral snakes, for example, have red, black and yellow bands all along their bodies. Imagine a Baryonyx that looked like that!

Feathers

New discoveries about dinosaur feathers are being made all the time. Recently, for example, it was found that dinosaurs developed feathers tens of millions of years earlier than we thought.

Jeholornis was a feathered dinosaur found in China, with a long tail a bit like a bird of paradise's. It lived 120 million years ago. Kulindadromeus was even older: it was running around in Siberia 160 million years ago, wearing a coat of fluffy feathers over most of its body.

SCIENCE FLASH

The ancestors of birds were feathered dinosaurs, but there were other kinds of dinosaur with feathers too. Experts think dinosaurs first developed feathers as a way of keeping themselves or their eggs warm. Later, their feathers may have also been used for trying to attract a mate or to scare off rivals.

Just you wait.

Baby T. rex – not so frightening with fluff

Yutyrannus was a huge predatory dinosaur from China. It was a bit smaller than T. rex.

T. REX

But that's not what made it less scary than I am ...

Fluffy feathers all over body

YUTYRANNUS

Fuzzy babies?

Some dinosaurs may have had a downy coating of feathers when they were young, then lost their feathers as they grew up.

Sails and spines

Several dinosaurs had a row of spines on their back. Sometimes the spines seem to have been for defence. Other spines had a 'sail' of skin between them. Experts are not 100 per cent sure what these sails were for.

Spinosaurus

The most famous spiny-sailed dinosaur is Spinosaurus – the biggest predatory dinosaur so far discovered, at about 14 m long and 12 tonnes. (T. rex could get to about 12 m long and weighed 6 tonnes.) Spinosaurus had almost twenty bony spines sticking up from its back, linked by skin to make a sail. At its highest, the sail was at least as tall as a grown man. But what was it for?

Hey there.

Maybe the sail was a way of attracting a mate. A bigger or brighter sail might have made you more popular back in Cretaceous times.

Brr, chilly this morning. Glad I've got my sail.

So ... hungry.

Spinosaurus ate mostly fish and spent a lot of time hunting in the water. Perhaps its sail stuck up in the sunlight and heated up the blood flowing through it.

The spines on Spinosaurus's back were so strong that some experts think they could have supported fat, which was stored there for when food was scarce.

Spear-backs

Large predatory dinosaurs liked to attack plant eaters by biting them on the back or neck. Spikes would have made this more difficult and dangerous.

Chungkingosaurus, for example, had two rows of flat spikes like giant spearheads sticking up all along its back and tail. These may have made a predatory Yangchuanosaurus think twice before attacking.

That'll teach you!

Ow! Ow, ow, ow! Not biting THAT guy again.

Circle of spikes

Kentrosaurus's main defence was a double row of sharp, bony spikes along its lower back and tail. It had a strong, very bendy tail, which it could move from side to side to stop attackers coming at it from behind.

Some experts think groups of Kentrosaurus might have defended themselves by forming a circle, with their spiky tails facing outwards.

Don't look at us, either!

Huddle up!

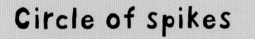

dinosaur guts

It's difficult to be sure how dinosaurs digested their food, because body bits like stomachs and intestines don't fossilise. Even so, experts have been able to work out quite a lot of facts about dinosaur digestion.

Did the dinosaur eat: **PLANTS** **MEAT**

BOOM.

YEUW!

We know dinosaurs pooed because they left the evidence behind. People have been digging up dinosaur poo - called coprolite - for over 150 years.

Coprolite contains lots of sulphur. In the past it has been used as fertiliser, and even to make explosives. Today, scientists are more interested in the information it gives us about what dinosaurs ate.

Biting and chewing

Some plant eaters, such as Diplodocus, had teeth that would have looked a bit like a garden rake. They were good for gathering food. Other plant eaters had teeth with a saw-like edge, which were good for shredding plants before they were swallowed.

Meat-eaters, such as Allosaurus, had teeth designed for biting or ripping chunks off their prey. Their teeth often broke or fell out. Fortunately, they were constantly growing new ones.

Stomachs and intestines

It takes a long time to extract nutrients from tough plants. The dinosaurs that ate them, such as the giant sauropods, may have processed their food in the same way as cows do today. They needed big stomachs (and maybe, like cows, more than one), where they could hold food while the nutrients were removed.

Meat is faster to digest compared to tough plants. Meat-eating dinosaurs would not have needed to keep food in their digestive system for long. Their stomachs and intestines could have been relatively small.

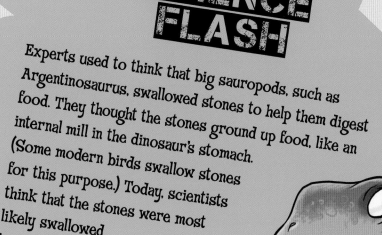

Not again.

SCIENCE FLASH

Experts used to think that big sauropods, such as Argentinosaurus, swallowed stones to help them digest food. They thought the stones ground up food, like an internal mill in the dinosaur's stomach. (Some modern birds swallow stones for this purpose.) Today, scientists think that the stones were most likely swallowed by accident.

I thought they were cookies ...

25

Hooting and honking

No one knows for sure what noises dinosaurs used to make. We are not even 100 per cent certain that they made any noise at all – but palaeontologists think it is likely.

*The most communicative lizards are geckos, which make chirrups, squeaks and clicks.

Skull clues

Fossilised skulls tell us about the noises some dinosaurs might have made. The lambeosaurs were a kind of dinosaur with bony head crests on their skulls. Inside was a system of air chambers. Some experts think these air chambers were a kind of trumpet.

Parasaurolophus was a lambeosaur with a long crest sticking backwards from the top of its head. Some experts think it pushed air through this to make a noise like a horn.

Other head-crest theories

Not everyone agrees that the lambeosaurs' head crests were trumpets. Some experts think the head crest helped lambeosaurs to recognise each other. (This would have been useful because there were several similar-looking dinosaurs around at the time.) Another theory is that the head crests were a way for lambeosaurs to control their temperature. To let cool or warm air flow through the crest, they just turned their head to the breeze.

The lambeosaurs were plant eaters and probably lived in herds. Being able to signal to each other would have been useful.

In 1998, a scientist and a palaeontologist used computer modelling of a Parasaurolophus crest to work out what it might have sounded like. They discovered that it would have made a very low noise, a bit like a foghorn.

snouts and sounds

The lambeosaurs are not the only dinosaurs that may have made sounds. Rhinorex and Gryposaurus both had long, fleshy snouts. (In fact, Rhinorex's name is a joke, meaning 'king of the noses'.) One idea about these is that the dinosaurs could have used them to honk out messages for the herd.

HOOO-OOONK!*

*Translation: "Look out, Teratophoneus about!"

27

The four freakiest dinosaurs?

Some dinosaurs had very freaky-looking body bits – but which were the freakiest of all? These four would all have a good chance of winning the prize.

Pegomastax

This dinosaur was only small: 60 cm from nose to tail, which made it about as big as a wallaby. But what it lacked in size, it made up for in freakiness. Pegomastax had a parrot-like beak, dog-like canine teeth in its lower jaw and a strip of quills a bit like a porcupine's sticking out of its back.

WINNER: OVERALL FREAKINESS

Pegomastax was probably a plant eater and used its teeth either for rooting up plants or defence.

Mamenchisaurus

Mamenchisaurus was an odd-looking sauropod. Its neck was about twice as long as its body, making this the giraffe of the dinosaur world. Palaeontologists think that, like giraffes, these dinosaurs might have wrapped their necks together while choosing a mate.

Neck: 12 m

Body: 6 m

WINNER: FREAKIEST NECK

Tail: 6 m

Mamenchisaurus fossils have been found that may belong to an animal weighing 75 tonnes. This would make it the largest land animal so far discovered.

Therizinosaurus

This dinosaur confused the first paleontologist to see it so much that he decided it must have been a 4.5-m turtle. The truth is even stranger. Therizinosaurus had a long neck and a pot belly. It may have been covered in feathers, which makes it sound a bit cuddly – but each hand was armed with three sword-like claws over a metre long.

WINNER:
FREAKIEST
FINGERS

Halszkaraptor

It looked a bit like a duck, or perhaps a swan, but Halszkaraptor was actually a dinosaur. It is SO freaky-looking that when it was first examined, experts thought it might have been joined together using bits of several different dinosaurs.

WINNER:
DINOSAUR THAT
DOESN'T LOOK
LIKE A
DINOSAUR

SCIENCE FLASH

When Halszkaraptor was examined in 2015, scientists used special scanners to create an image of the whole fossil without breaking it out of its rocky case. They were checking that the fossil was not made of bits from more than one dinosaur. The scan also showed that Halszkaraptor had pressure sensors in its face, which would have helped it sense prey in the water.

Glossary

binocular vision seeing with two eyes that both face forwards, so that what you can see with one eye overlaps with what you can see with the other. Predators often have binocular vision, because it helps them see how far away things are and this makes it easier to hunt.

computer modelling use of a computer to work out what something may look like or how it could work

Cretaceous period of time between roughly 150 million and 66 million years ago. This was when dinosaurs ruled the Earth, which they shared with other animals, such as birds, mammals and pterosaurs.

digest take nutrients (which provide living things with energy, and help them grow and repair themselves) from food

digestive system parts of the body that take nutrients from food. These include the stomach and intestines.

evolve change over time to better suit the place where you live or the food you eat. For example, animals that live in cold places usually evolve a thick coat or some other way of keeping warm.

Jurassic period of time between roughly 201 million and 150 million years ago. When the Jurassic began, archosaurs ruled, but by the end dinosaurs had begun to take over.

mate member of the opposite sex with whom young are produced

nocturnal awake and active mostly at night

palaeontologist scientist who studies fossilised animals and plants

Pangaea huge 'supercontinent', a giant area of land that existed on Earth between roughly 335 and 175 million years ago. Pangaea then broke up, eventually forming the continents we know today.

pressure sensor place on the skin that is especially good at sensing nearby moving objects

pupil dark area at the centre of an eye, which gets bigger or smaller to let in more or less light

reptile animal that has a backbone and four limbs (or had four-limbed ancestors). Reptiles usually produce young by laying eggs on land. Today's reptiles include turtles, crocodiles, snakes and lizards.

sauropod large (or giant) plant-eating dinosaur with a long neck and tail, small head, large body and thick, strong legs

species group of animals or plants that look similar, have the same body bits and are able to have young with each other

stance how a person or animal stands – for example, standing with your feet wide apart is a wide stance

vocalise make a sound from inside your own body. So, speaking, barking or purring are all vocalising: banging a drum, scratching at the door or rolling over and looking cute are not.

Sorry, I don't bark ...

Finding out more

Books to read

Anyone upset that there weren't more fun number-facts about dinosaurs in this book shouldn't worry – just head for the library and take out a copy of:

The Big Countdown: 34.7 Quadrillion Minutes Since The Last Dinosaur Died
Paul Mason (Franklin Watts, 2018)

For simple facts about almost every dinosaur, a good reference book is:

Dictionary of Dinosaurs: An Illustrated A–Z Of Every Dinosaur Ever Discovered
Dr Matthew G Baron and Dieter Braun
(Wide-Eyed Editions, 2018)

If you'd like to know more about which dinosaurs may have battled each other millions of years ago (and where), these four books in the 'When Dinosaurs Ruled' series will fascinate you:

Hunters In The Forest, Slayers By The Shore, Predators On The Plains and *Stalkers In The Swamp*
Paul Mason (Hungry Tomato, 2018/19)

If you're REALLY into dinosaurs and prepared to work hard, one of the best reference books around is an adult book:

The Princeton Field Guide to Dinosaurs
Gregory S Paul (Princeton University Press, 2016)

Places to visit

In London, the best place to visit to find out about dinosaurs is:

The Natural History Museum, Cromwell Road, London SW7 5BD
www.nhm.ac.uk

Other great dinosaur/natural history museums in the UK include:

Dorset County Museum and Dinosaur Museum, both in Dorchester
www.dorsetcountymuseum.org and
www.thedinosaurmuseum.com

Oxford University Museum of Natural History, Oxford
www.ox.ac.uk

Manchester Museum, Manchester where the star attraction is Stan the T-rex
www.museum.manchester.ac.uk

World Museum, Liverpool
www.liverpoolmuseums.org.uk/world-museum

Kelvingrove Art Gallery and Museum, housed in a beautiful building in Glasgow
www.glasgowlife.org.uk/museums#venues

Index

archosaurs 10

birds 8, 10, 15, 17 –19, 21, 25, 28–29
Bolt, Usain 11
brachiosaurs 15 (and see individual species)
brains 14–15, 26

clubs (on tails) 8–9, 12
coprolite 24
crests 26–27

defence, adapted for 5, 8–9, 12–13, 22–23, 28
diet 4–7 , 19, 22, 24–25
digestion 24–25
dinosaurs (individual species)
    Afrovenator 5
    Albertosaurus 17
    Aletopelta 12
    Allosaurus 10–11, 25
    Animantarx 12
    Ankylosaurus 7 , 9, 13
    Apatosaurus 10
    Archaeopteryx 18–19
    Argentinosaurus 11, 25
    Baryonyx 5, 20
    Brachiosaurus 5
    Chungkingosaurus 23
    Coahuilaceratops 8
    Compsognathus 11
    Deinonychus 11, 16
    Diplodocus 25
    Euoplocephalus 12
    Gastonia 13
    Gorgosaurus 17
    Gryposaurus 27
    Halszkaraptor 29
    Hoplitosaurus 12
    Jeholornis 21
    Kentrosaurus 23
    Kosmoceratops 5, 8–9
    Kulindadromeus 21

Mamenchisaurus 28
Masiakasaurus 6
Mei long 15
Microraptor 19
Nigersaurus 7
Ornithomimus 5
Parasaurolophus 26–27
Pegomastax 28
Pentaceratops 8
Procompsognathus 15
Rhinorex 27
Saichania 13
Sauropelta 13
Sinosauropteryx 20
Spinosaurus 5–6, 22
Spinostropheus 5
Stegosaurus 10, 14
Tarchia 10
Teratophoneus 27
Therizinosaurus 29
Torosaurus 8
Triceratops 7 –8, 15
Troodon 14
Tyrannosaurus rex (T. rex)
    6, 9, 11, 17 , 21–23
Velociraptor 15–16
Yangchuanosaurus 23
Yi qi 19
Yutyrannus 21

eyes 15–17

feathers 8, 18–21, 29
flight 18–19

guts 24–25

hips 10
horns 5, 8–10

intelligence 14–15

lambeosaurs 26–27
    (and see individual species)
legs 5, 10–11, 19

mates, attracting 8, 21–22, 28
mobility 5, 10–11

noise, making 26–27

ornithischians 10 (and see individual species)
osteoderms 12

palaentologists 12, 18–19, 26–29
Pangaea 4
plates, bony 12–13

reptiles 10, 12, 15, 17 , 20, 26
rings, scleral 16

saurischians 10 (and see individual species)
sauropods 5, 25, 28
    (and see individual species)
sails 5, 22
sensors, pressure 6, 29
skin 12–13, 19–22
    armour 10, 12–13
    spikes 8, 13, 23
    spines 22–23
sleep 15
stegosaurs 15 (and see individual species)

teeth 5–7 , 12, 25, 28
theropods 5, 17 (and see individual species)
titanosaurs 11, 14 (and see individual species)
tyrannosaurs 6, 8, 13, 15, 17
    (and see individual species)

vision 16–17
vocalisation 26–27

weight 4
wings 18–19